KELTIC ALPHABET COLORING 2

Capital Letters

Kathy O'Meara

Perelandra Design

This "Keltic Alphabet Coloring 2: Capital Letters" Book contains contains drawings of 26 framed Capital Letters (A-Z) inspired by figures from the Book of Kells. These letters, with their whimsical characters, will delight Children of any age. Each page has 8"x10" guidelines for cutting and framing your finished masterpiece.

Books by Kathy O'Meara

Keltic Crosses Coloring
Keltic Crosses Coloring 2
Keltic Alphabet Coloring: Capital Letters
Keltic Alphabet Coloring: Lower Case Letters
Keltic Coloring: Knots & Numbers
Keltic Coloring: Knotted Nature
Keltic Alphabet Coloring 2: Capital Letters
Keltic Alphabet Coloring 2: Lower Case Letters
Keltic Creatures For Kids
Keltic Creatures For Kids 2
Keltic Knots For Kids

Stained Glass "Window" Patterns

Spring Flowers
Summer Flowers
Autumn
Circle of Life
Keltic Christian

International Standard Book Number

ISBN-13: 978-1724624918
ISBN-10: 1724624911

U

www.ingramcontent.com/pod-product-compliance
Lightning Source LLC
Chambersburg PA
CBHW080045260726
48658CB00007B/2742